HAPPY THANKSGIVING

COLORING BOOKS FOR KIDS AGES 4-8

SIMPLE BIG PICTURES HAPPY HOLIDAY COLORING BOOKS FOR TODDLERS AND PRESCHOOLERS

The Coloring Book Art Design Studio

THANKSGIVING

COLORING BOOKS FOR KIDS AGES 4-8

by The Coloring Book Art Design Studio

THANKSGIVING
COLORING BOOKS FOR KIDS AGES 4-8

THIS BOOK
BELONG TO

____

____

LET'S TEST YOUR COLOR

AUTUMN FESTIVAL
HAPPY
Thanksgiving

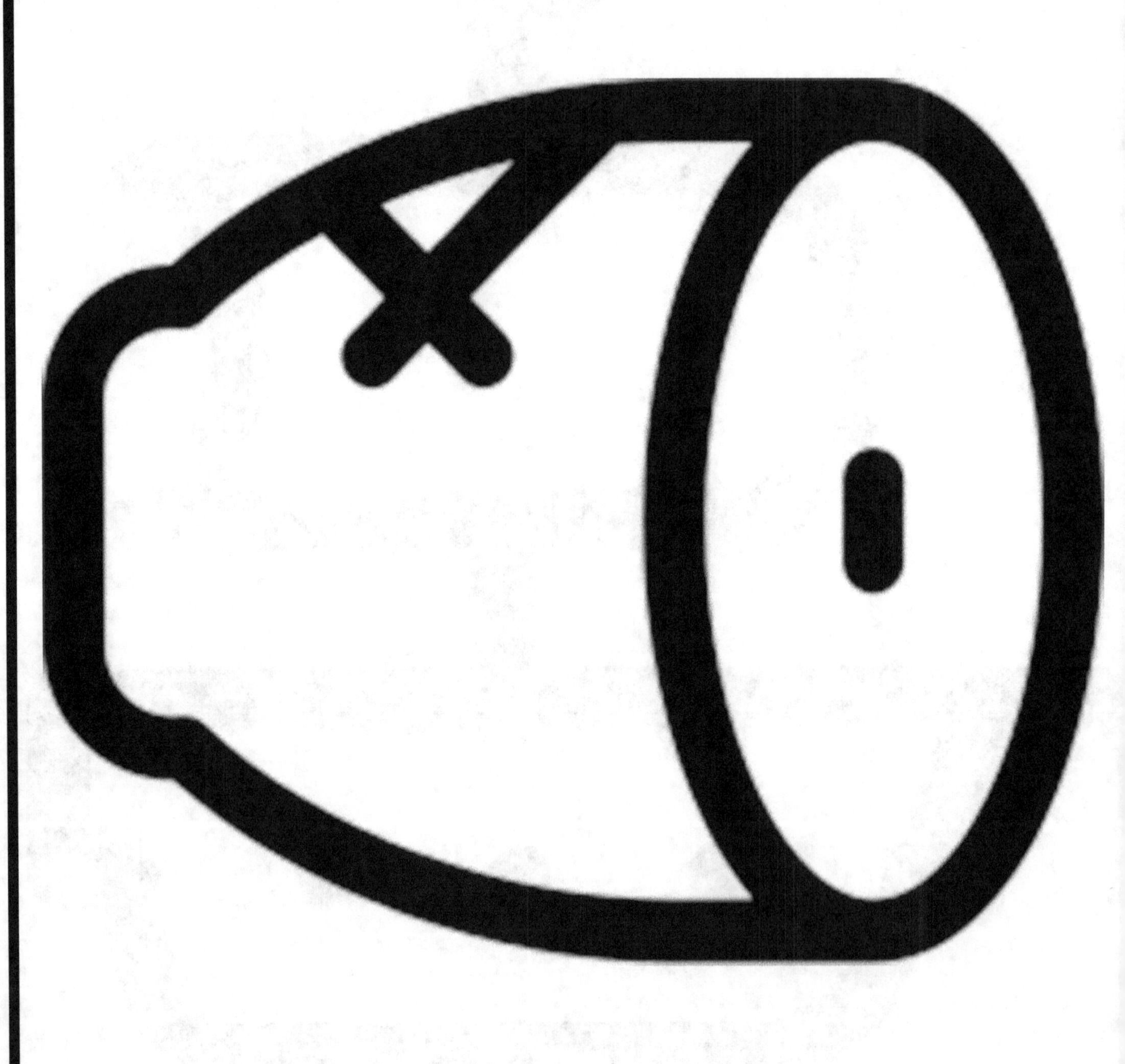

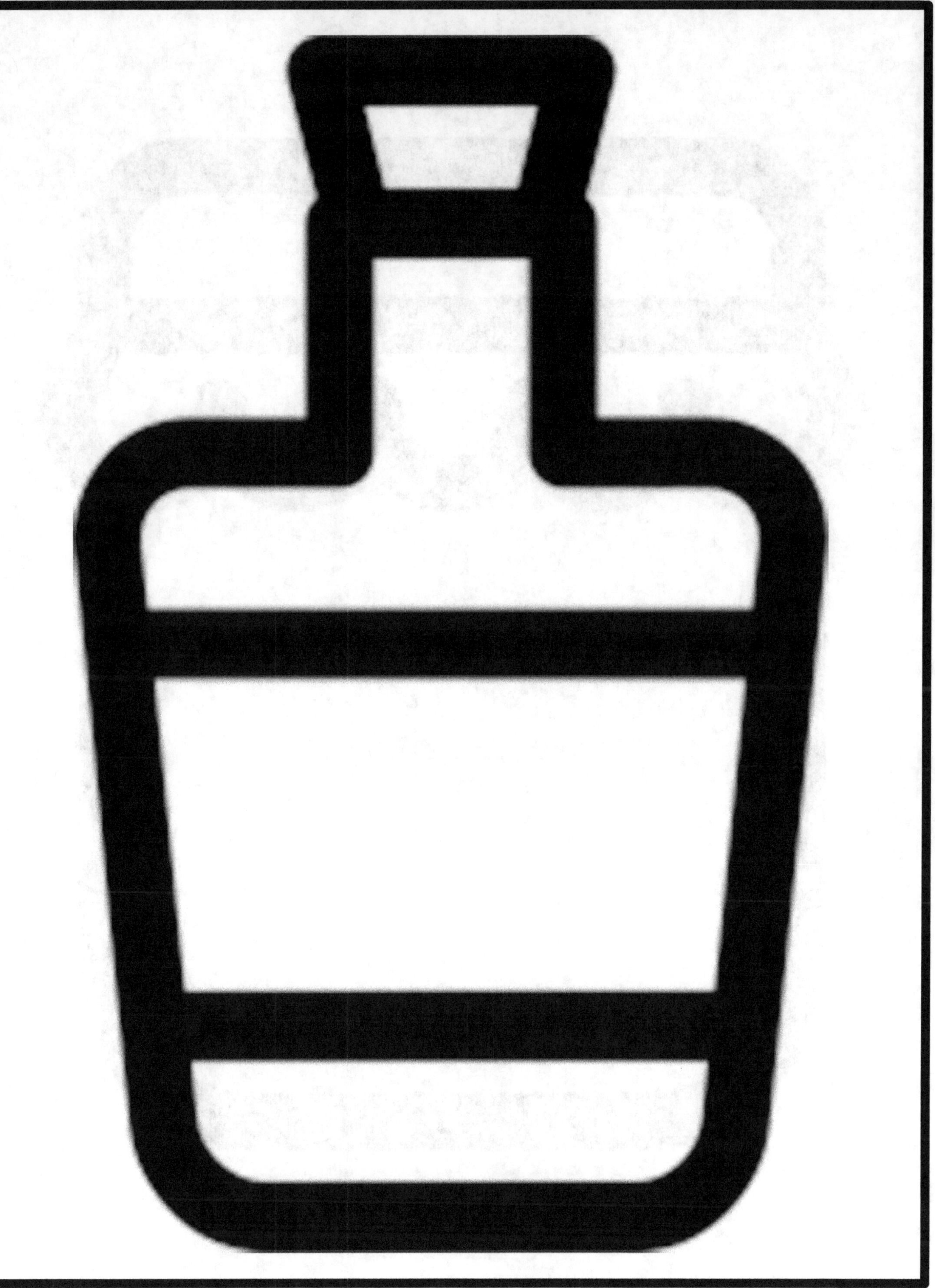

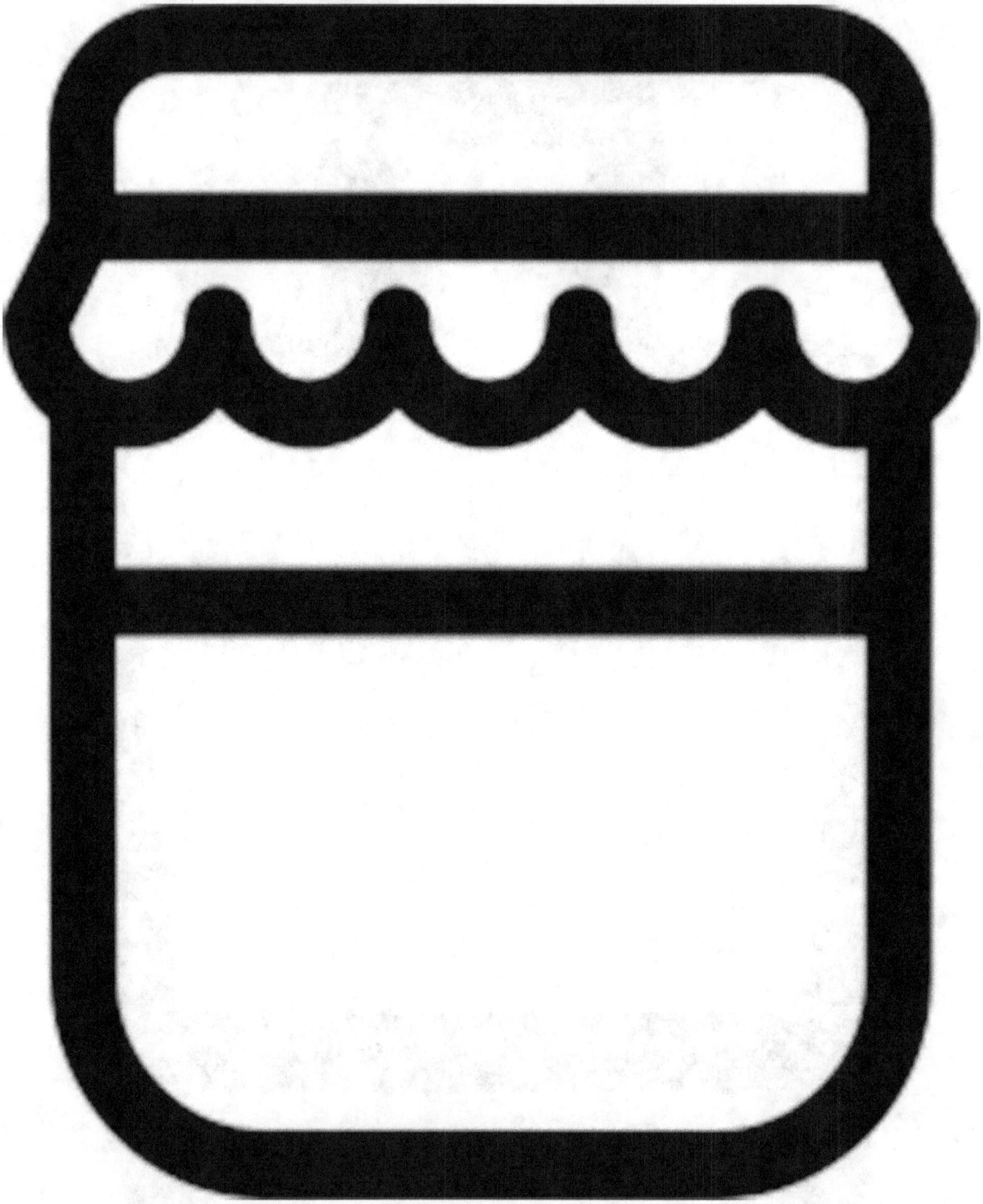

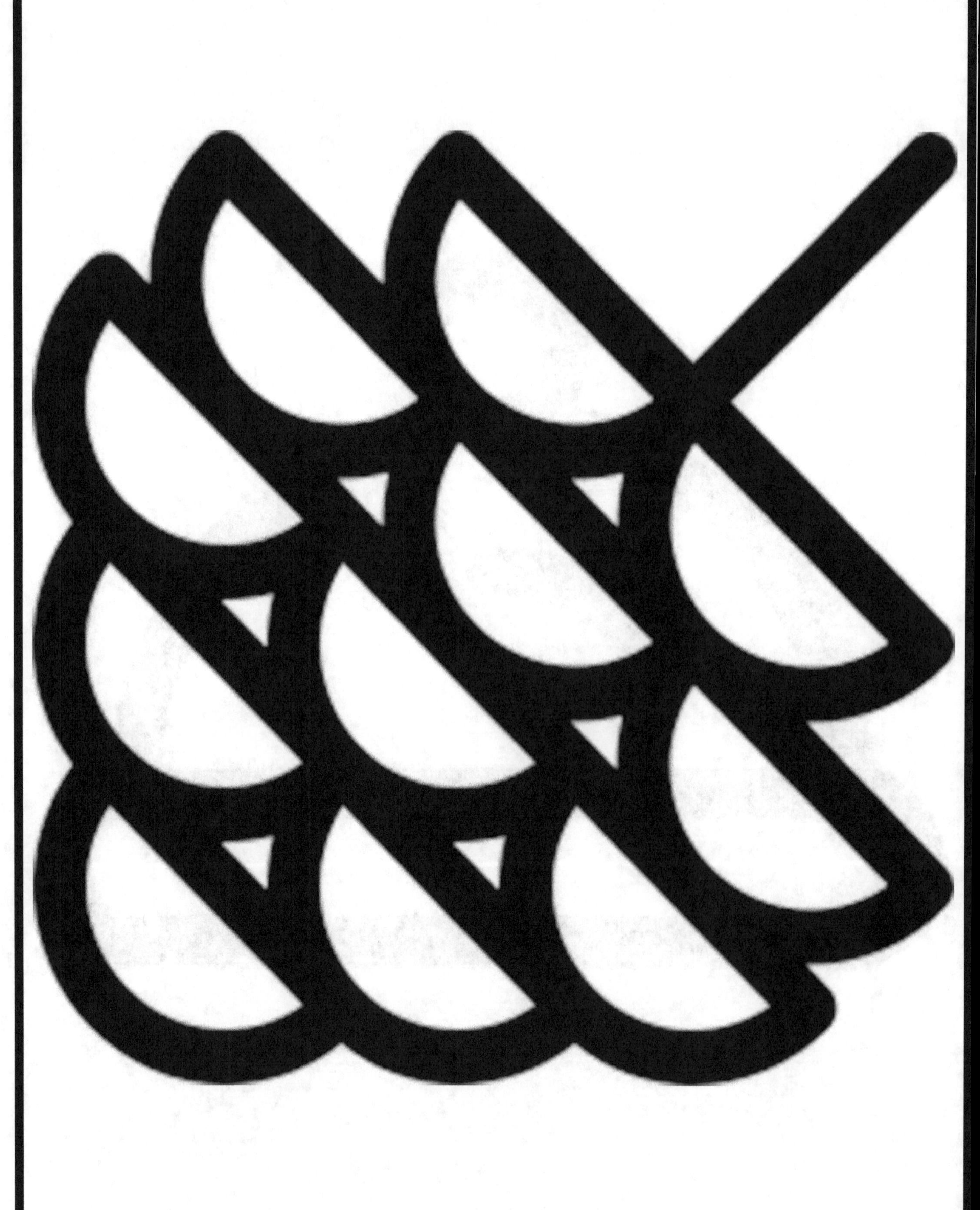

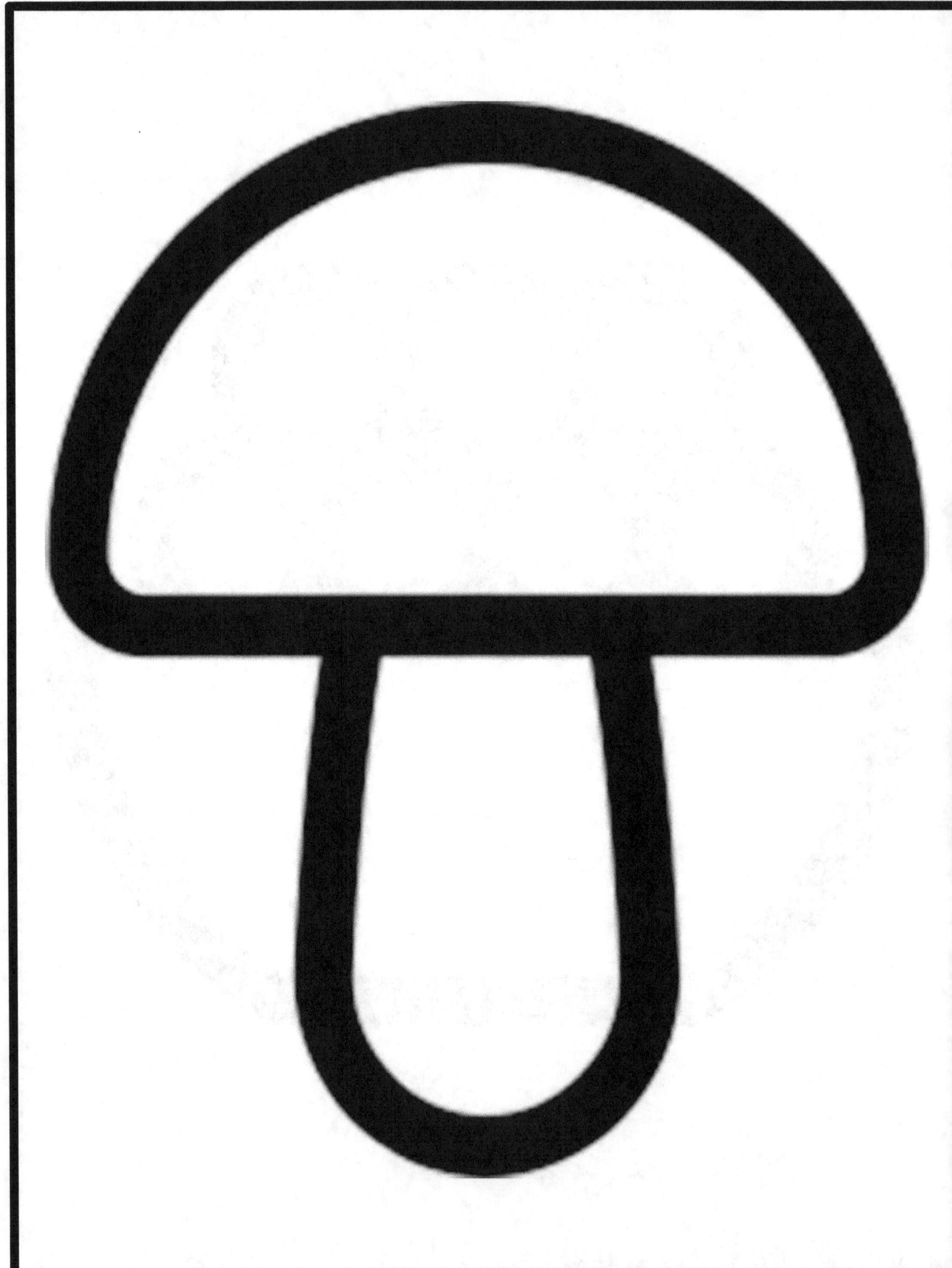

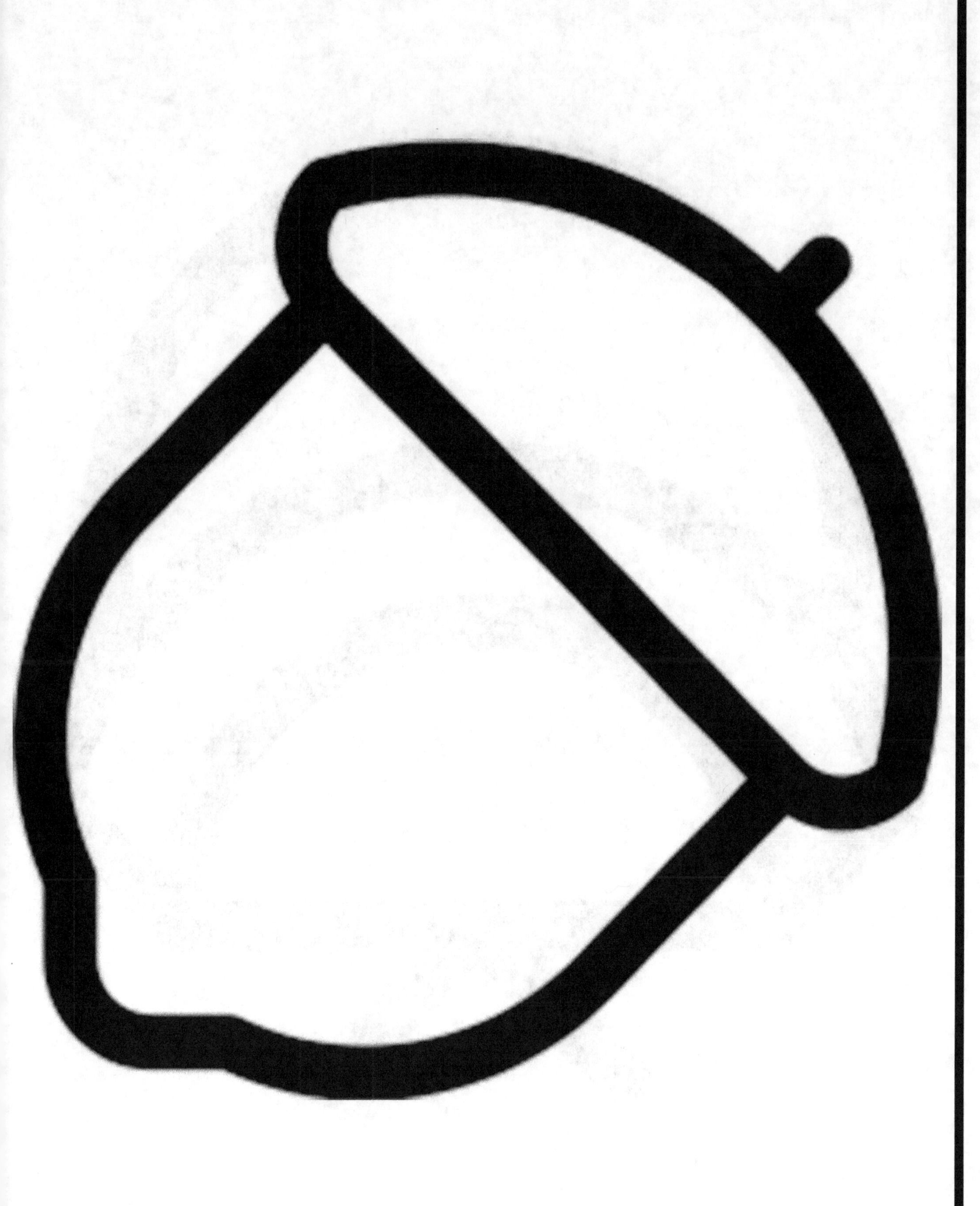

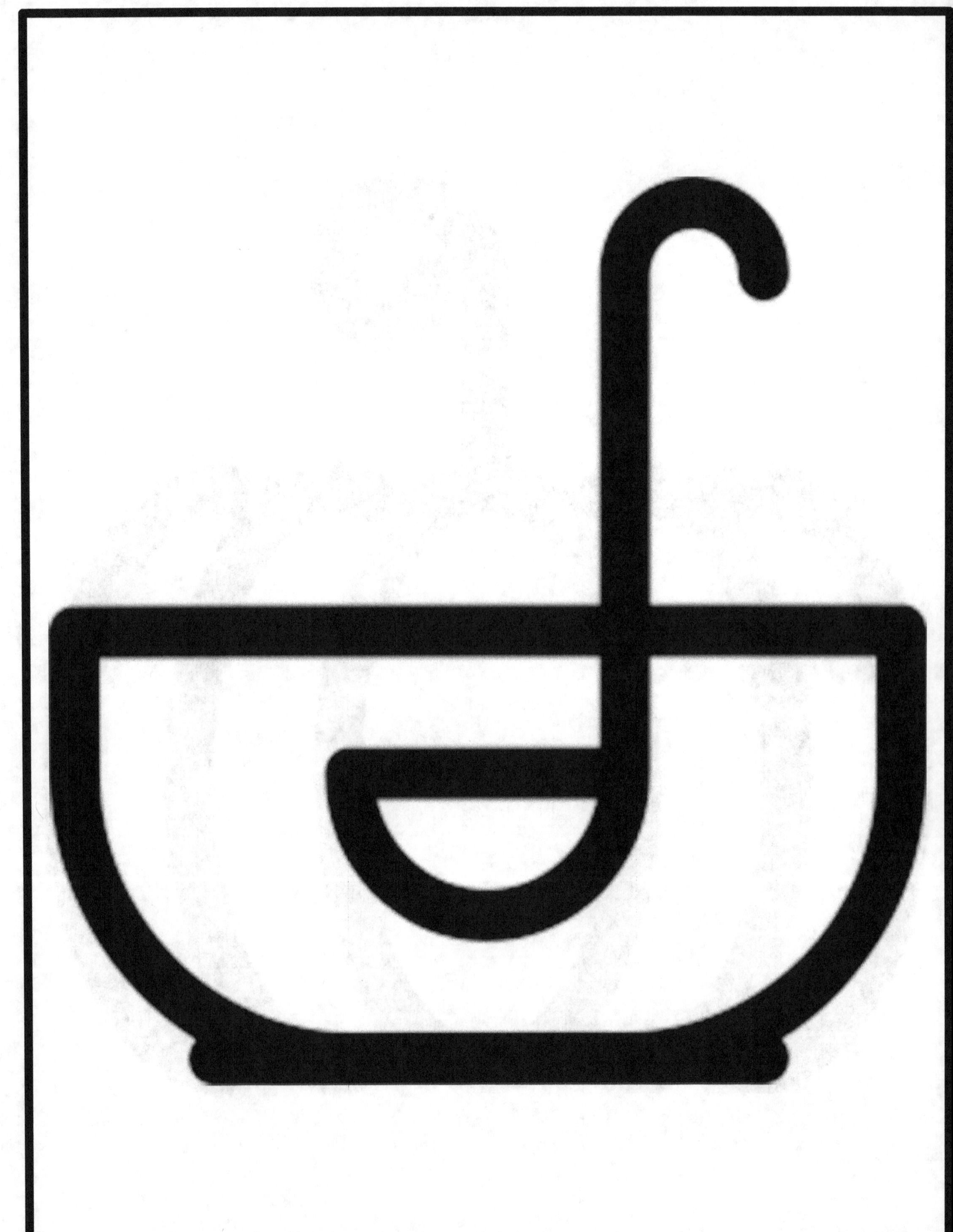

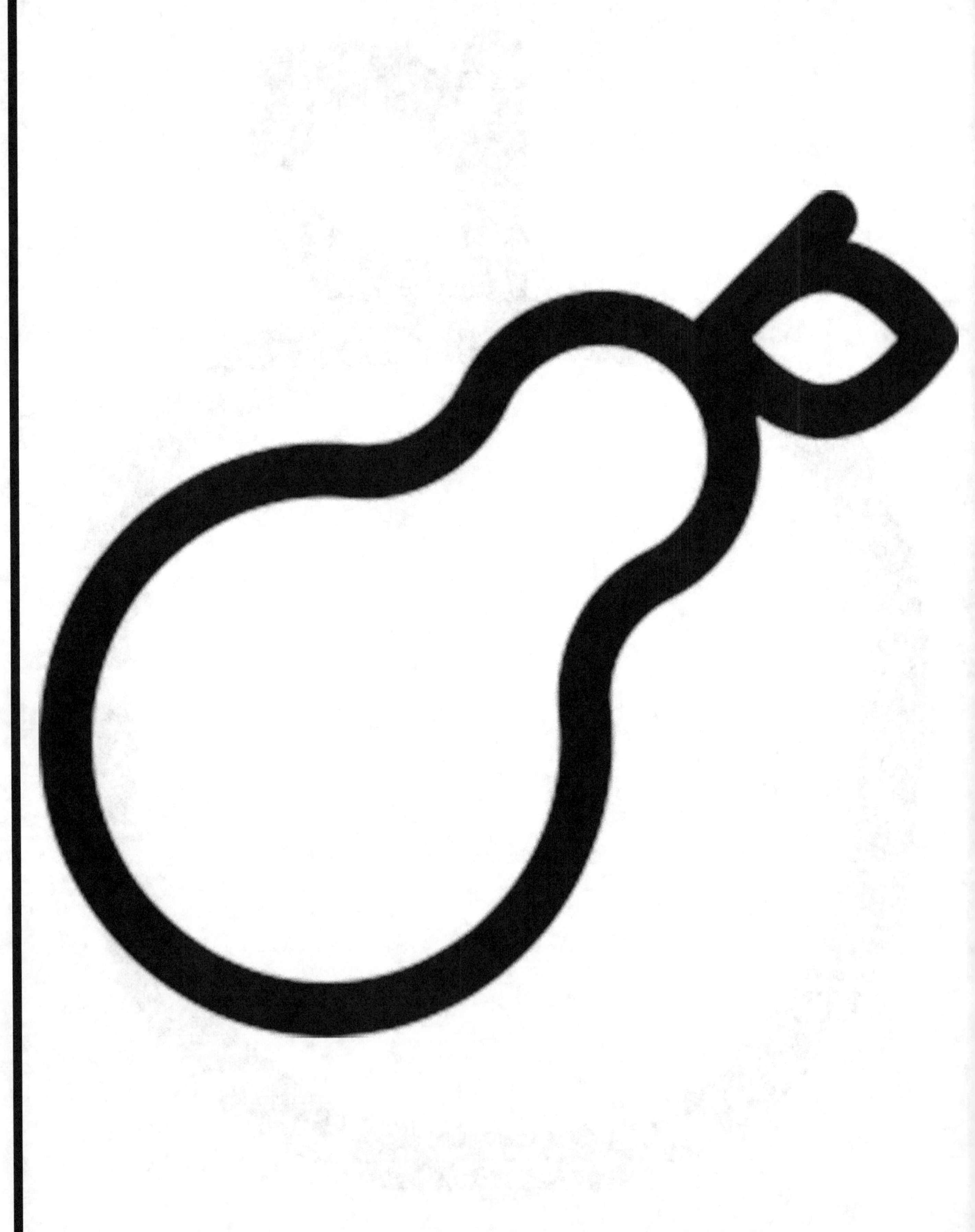

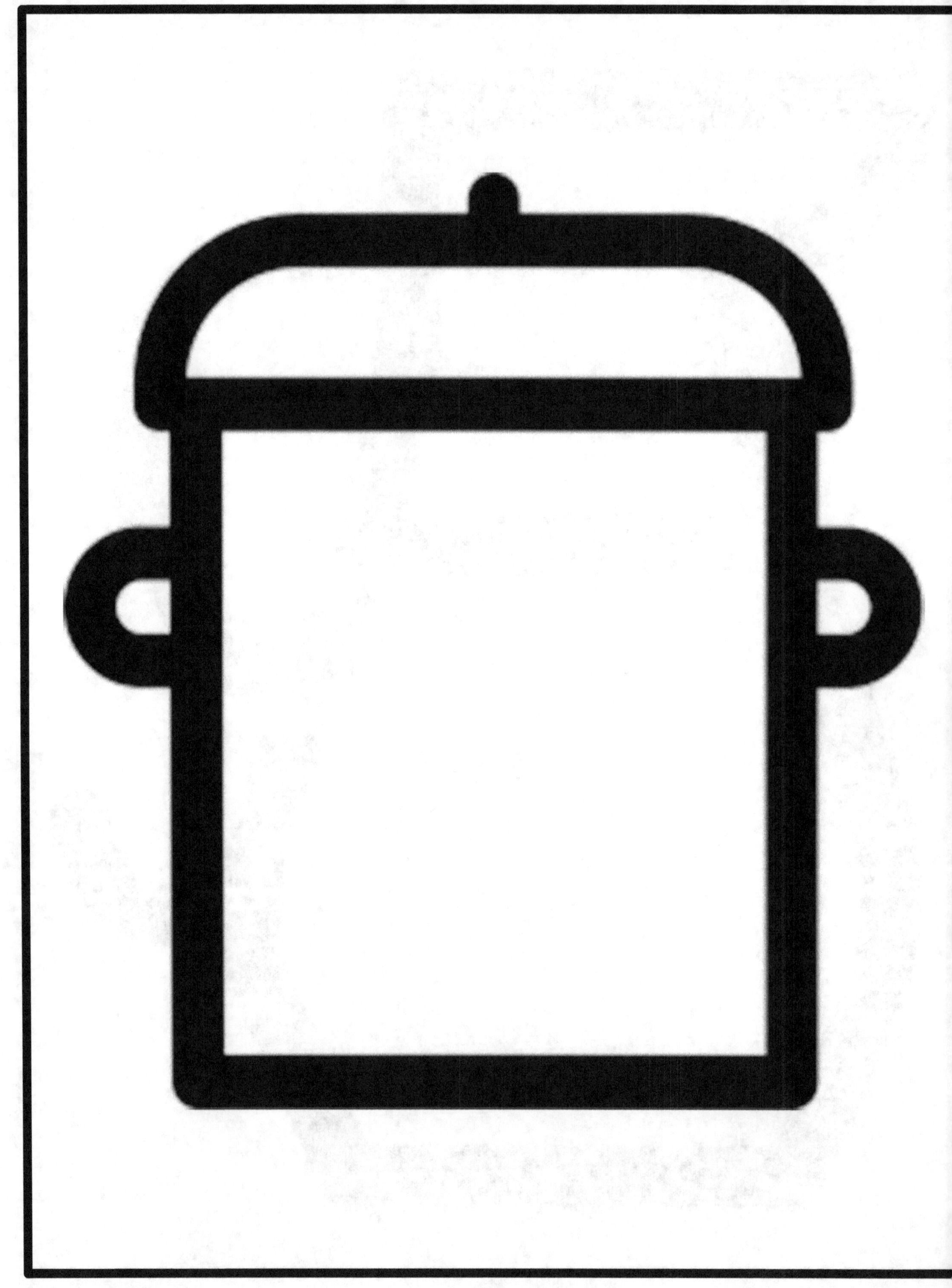

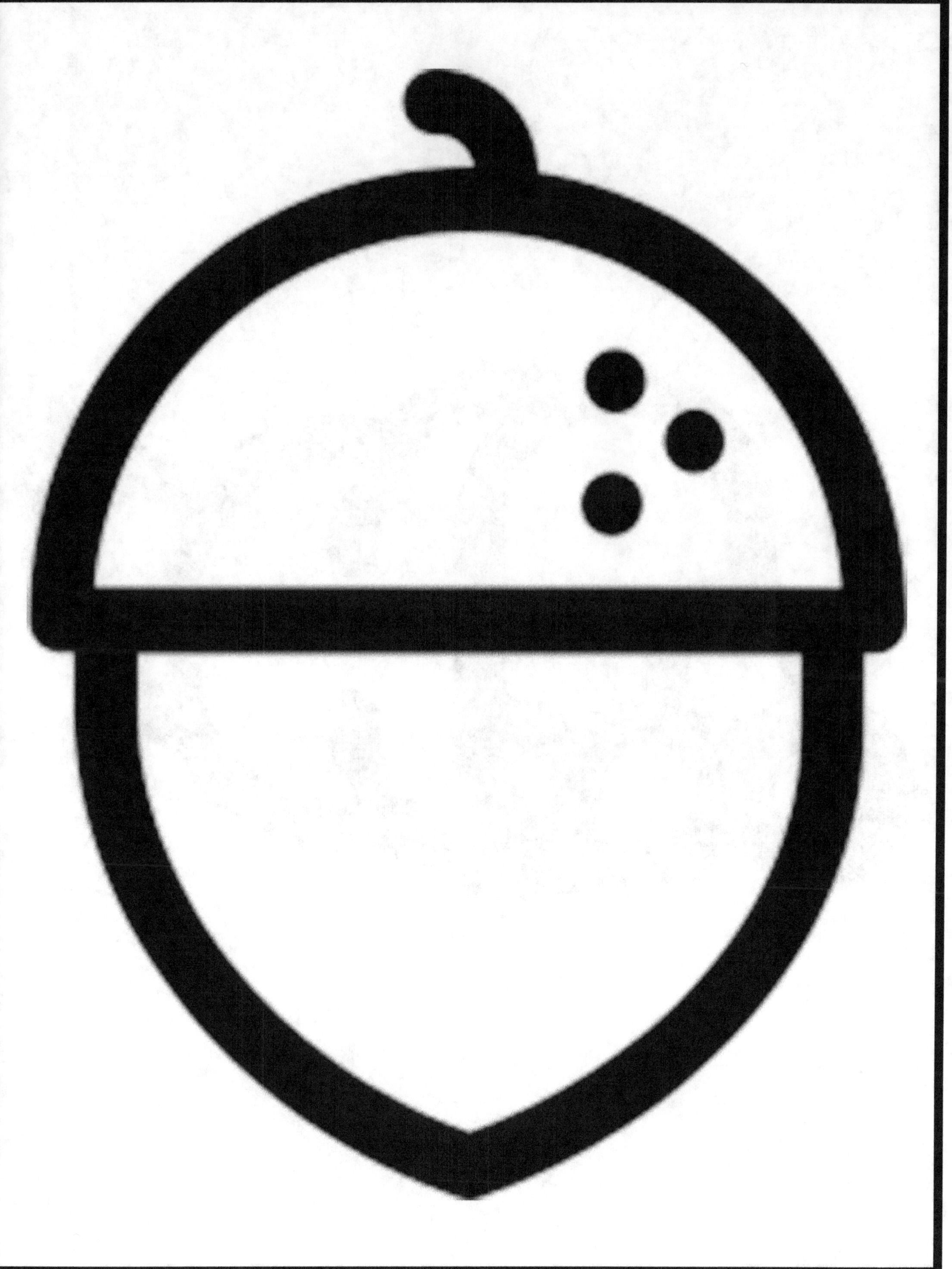

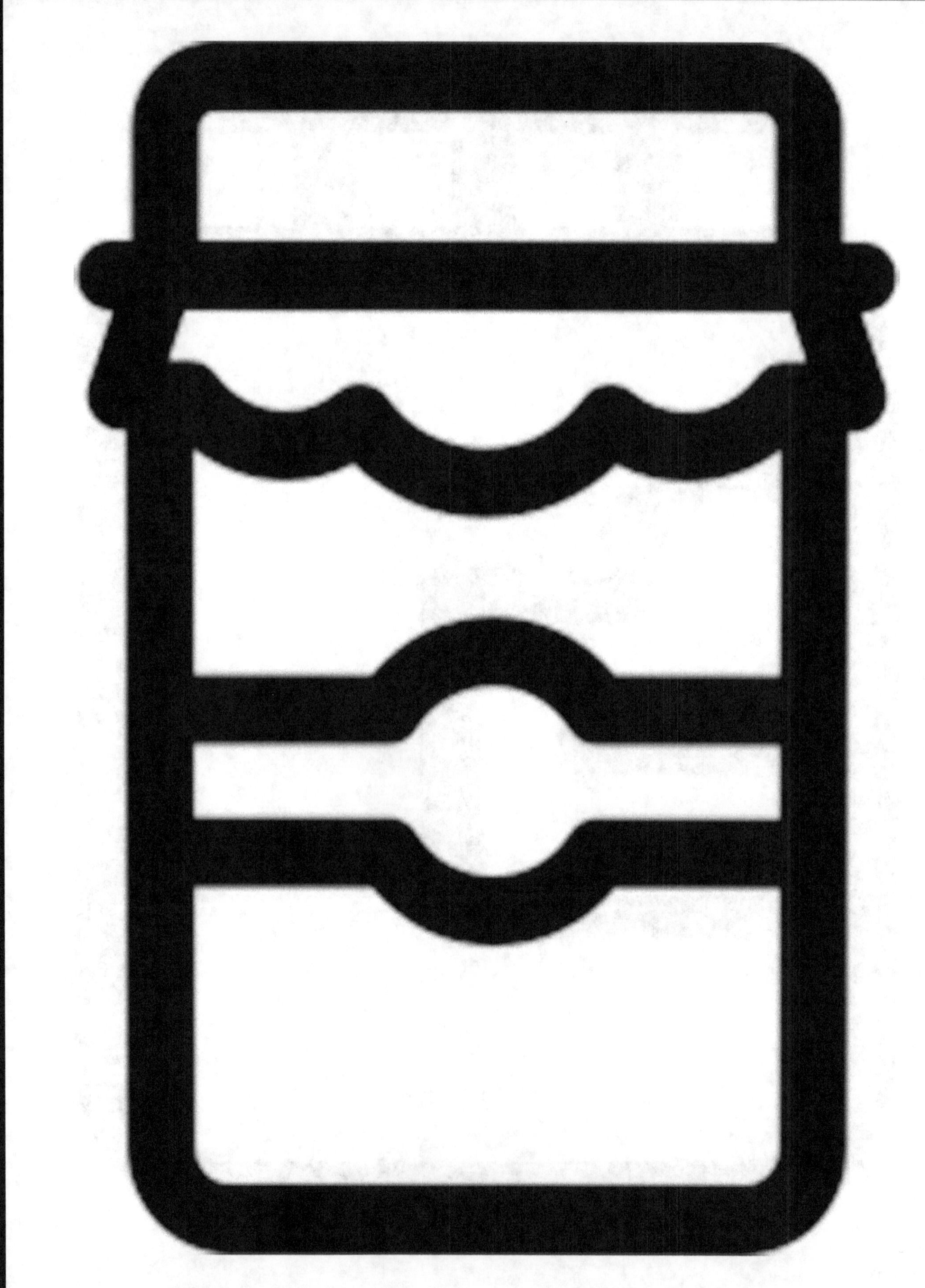

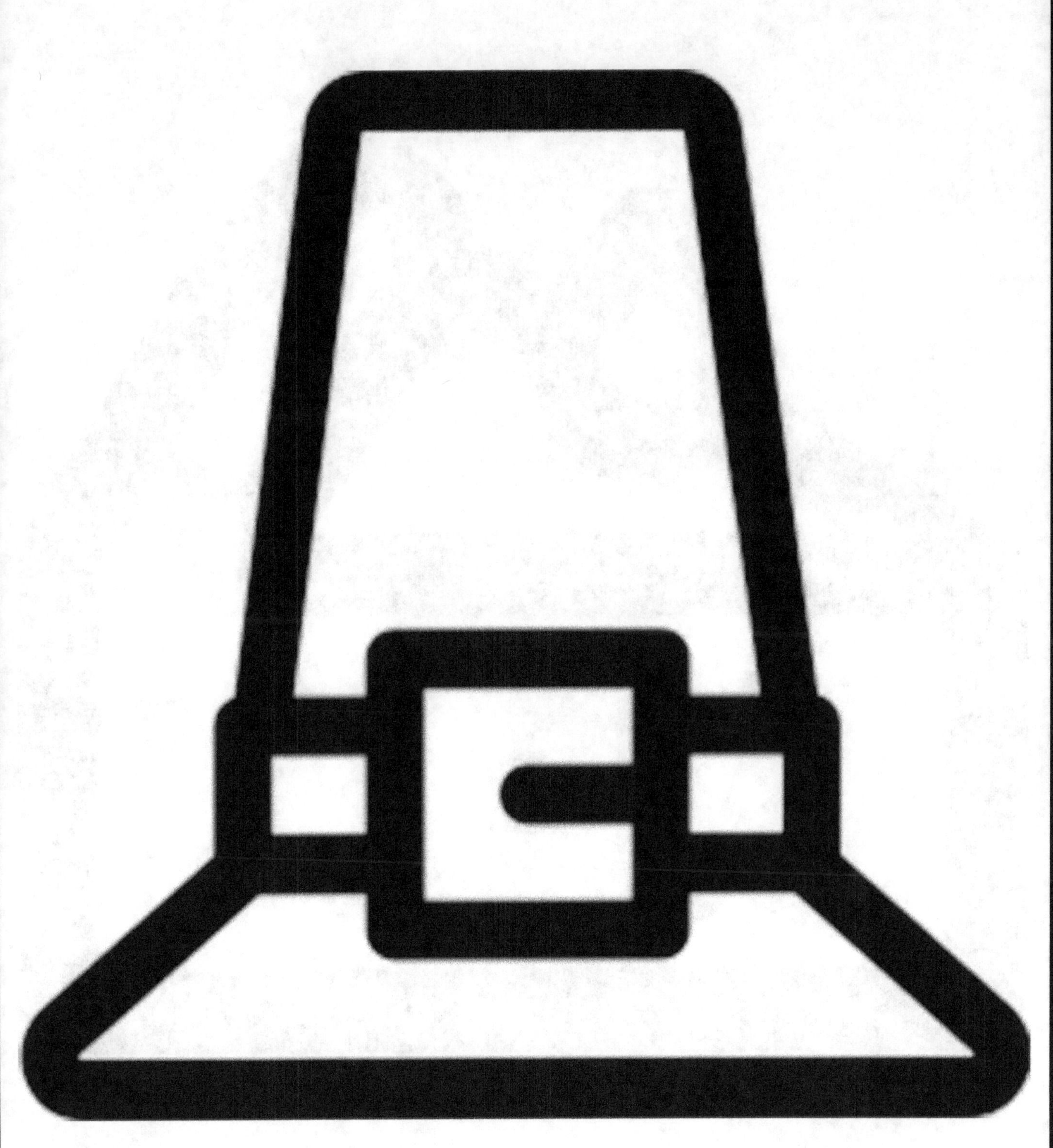

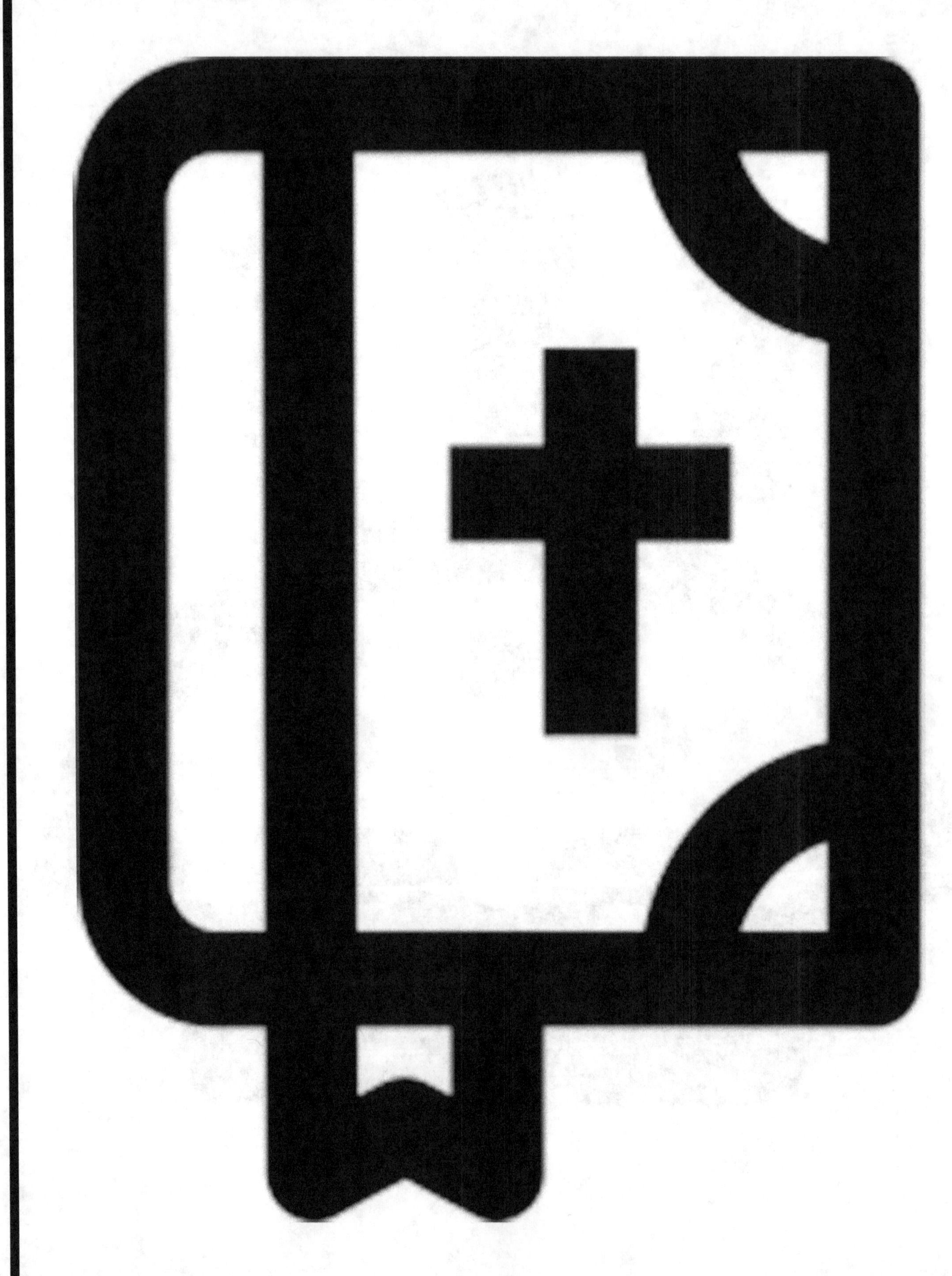

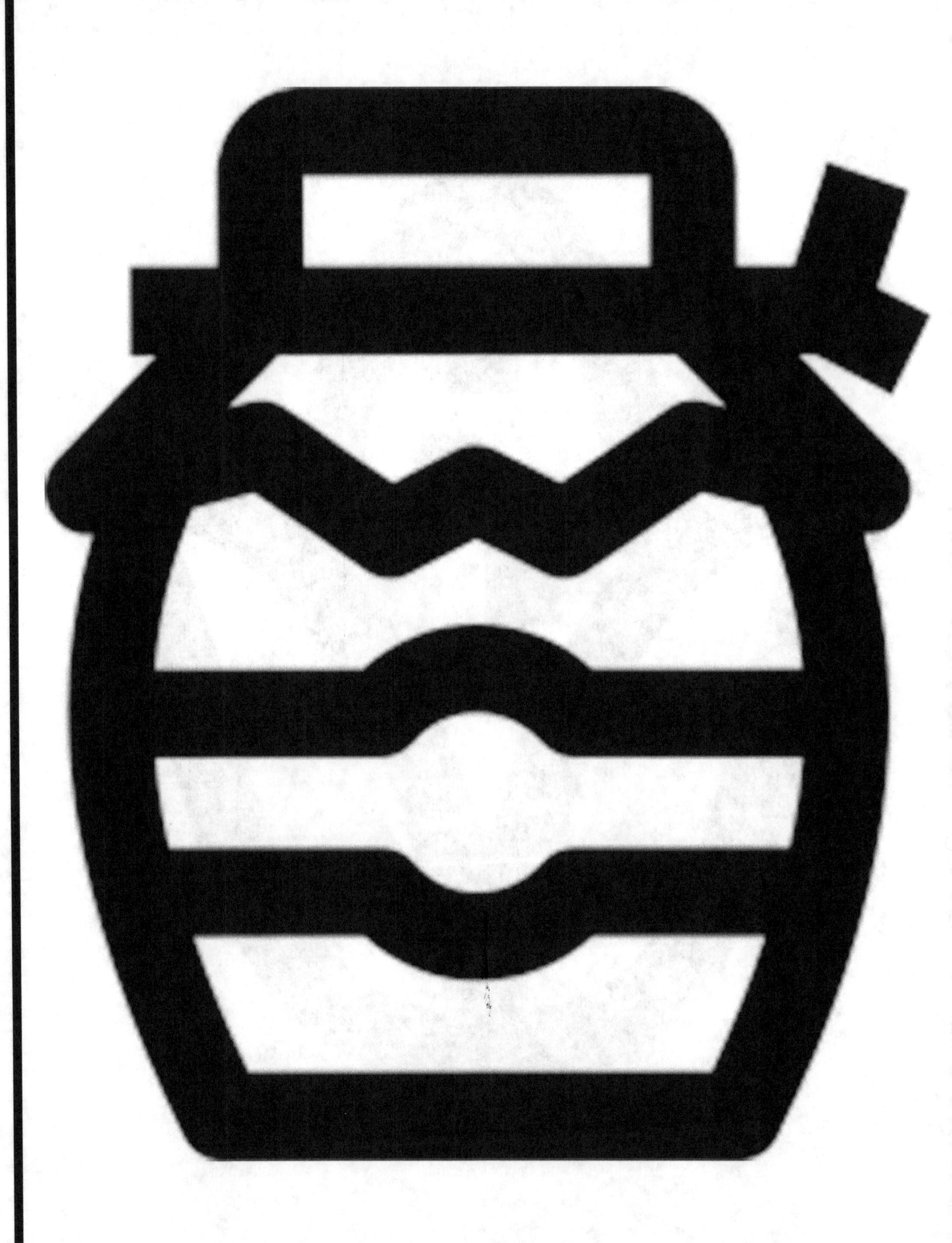

THANK
YOU